Apples are absolutely appetizing.

Beautiful butterflies were once...

...caterpillars covered in cocoons.

C c

David's dog loves to dig.

Every elephant has enormous ears.

Fred is a fearless firefighter.

Guess who just got a grooming.

Henry hopped on top of his horse.

Iris is ill and itching because of an insect bite.

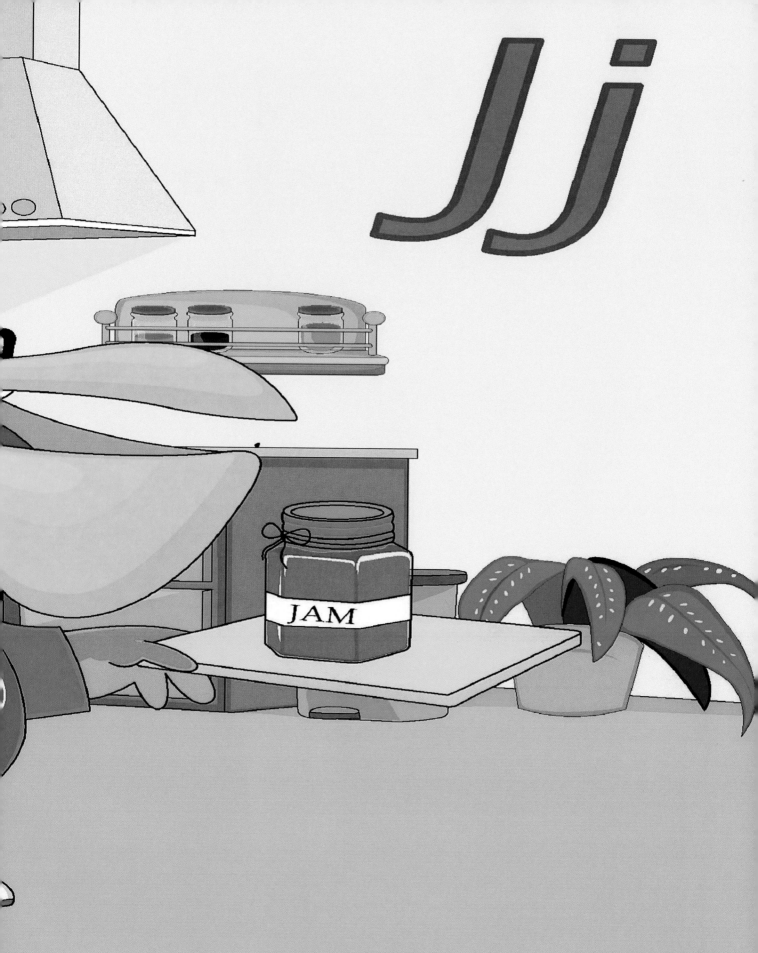

Jelly or jam?

Kenji's favorite part of karate is kicking.

Lydia loaned Lana some loose leaf paper.

Mayonnaise and mustard.

Nothing but net!

Other than the owl, Owen's favorite bird is the osprey.

Picou Pelican prepared a pitcher of pineapple punch.

Quit quarreling over Queenie's quilt.

Rocky was rewarded a red remote controlled racecar.

Sara is saving money so she can sail to South Africa.

Timmy, Tasha, and Terrance played Twister.

Ursula's umbrella is rather unique.

Vince's imagination is very vivid.

What would we do without water?

Xavier plays the xylophone.

Yy

You shouldn't yawn without covering your mouth.

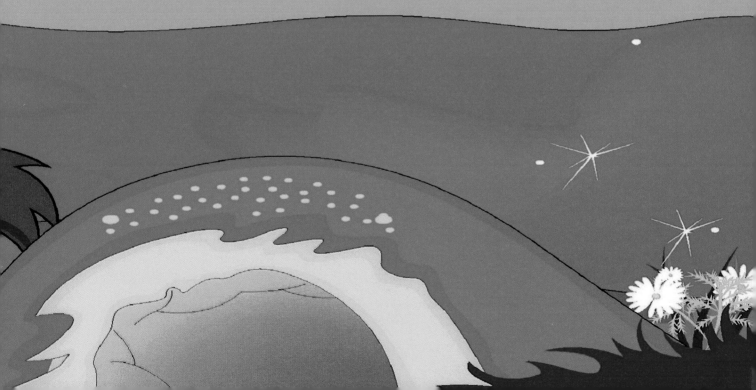

Zoya fed a zebra at the zoo.